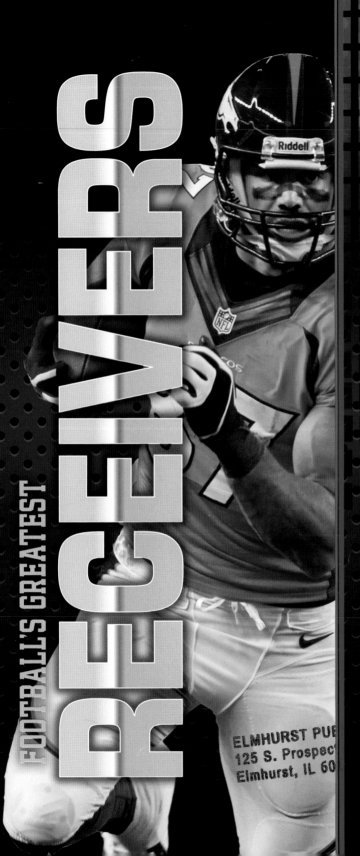

FOOTBALL'S GREATEST
RECEIVERS

Sports Illustrated KIDS

BY ERIC BRAUN

CAPSTONE PRESS
a capstone imprint

ELMHURST PUB
125 S. Prospect
Elmhurst, IL 60

Sports Illustrated Kids Football's Greatest are published by Capstone Press,
1710 Roe Crest Drive, North Mankato, Minnesota 56003
www.capstonepub.com

Library of Congress Cataloging-in-Publication Data
Cataloging information on file with the Library of Congress
ISBN 978-1-4914-0760-8 (library binding)

Editorial Credits
Brenda Haugen, editor; Heidi Thompson, designer; Eric Gohl, media researcher;
Gene Bentdahl, production specialist

Photo Credits
Sports Illustrated: Al Tielemans, 4l, 8, 13, 26, 27r, Bill Frakes, 7bl, Bob Rosato, 22, Damian Strohmeyer, 5,
18–19, 27l, David E. Klutho, cover, 10b, 12l, 20, 21r, John Biever, 9, 14t, 15, 19r, John W. McDonough, 6,
12r, 16, 17l, 21l, 28l, Peter Read Miller, 7t, 24, 25, Robert Beck, 1, 7br, 10t, 11l, 11r, 17r, 28r, 29, Simon Bruty,
4r, 14b, 23l, 23r

Printed in China by Nordica
0414/CA21400595
032014   008095NORDF14

*All statistics are through the 2013 season.

MARQUES COLSTON

The New Orleans Saints faced a tough matchup against the San Francisco 49ers in a 2012 divisional playoff game. The Saints were down by 10 points in the final minutes of the first half. Saints receiver Marques Colston lined up wide right, and quarterback Drew Brees took the **snap** from the **shotgun** position.

Colston stormed off the line, got around the cornerback, and sprinted downfield. Brees lofted a perfect pass, and Colston caught it in stride, landing one foot easily in bounds. He made sure to touch his other foot in the end zone as he tumbled over the orange pylon. Touchdown, New Orleans Saints!

Year	Team	Games	Yards	Yds/Game	Yds/Catch	Receiving TDs
2006	NO	14	1,038	74.1	14.8	8
2007	NO	16	1,202	75.1	12.3	11
2008	NO	11	760	69.1	16.2	5
2009	NO	16	1,074	67.1	15.3	9
2010	NO	15	1,023	68.2	12.2	7
2011	NO	14	1,143	81.6	14.3	8
2012	NO	16	1,154	72.1	13.9	10
2013	NO	15	943	62.9	12.6	5

The Saints took Hofstra University's Marques Colston in the seventh round of the 2006 NFL **draft**. He became a starter right away, setting the NFL record for most catches in a player's first two years with 168. In 2007 he scored a career-high 11 touchdowns. After the 2009 season, Colston helped the Saints to a Super Bowl victory with seven catches for 83 yards.

Colston has been a pass-catching machine for Brees. He's had more than 1,000 yards receiving six of his eight seasons in the NFL. He nearly had another 1,000-yard season in 2013 and helped his team to the division playoffs.

snap—the act of the center putting the football in play from the line of scrimmage
shotgun—the position from which the quarterback receives the ball a few feet behind
   the line of scrimmage instead of taking it directly from the center's hands
draft—the system by which NFL teams select new players

MICHAEL CRABTREE

The San Francisco 49ers took on the Green Bay Packers in a 2012 playoff game—the first playoff game for 49ers quarterback Colin Kaepernick. Wide receiver Michael Crabtree didn't let his quarterback down. Early in the second quarter, down 14-7, the 49ers faced third and 12 at the Green Bay 12-yard line. Kaepernick spotted Crabtree and threw a short pass down the middle. Crabtree extended his arms for the catch and ran the remaining nine yards for the touchdown. During the Packers' next drive, the 49ers' defense quickly shut them down. Kaepernick got the ball back less than two minutes after Crabtree's first touchdown. The 49ers marched up the field to the 20-yard line. Kaepernick went back to Crabtree, who caught the ball and fell across the goal line with his defender draped all over him. Score, 49ers!

Crabtree made a huge impact at Texas Tech University. In 2007 and 2008, he earned the Fred Biletnikoff Award as the nation's top college receiver. San Francisco picked Crabtree 10th overall in the 2009 draft. He became a better player each year, increasing his receiving yards in his second and third NFL seasons. In his fourth season, when Colin Kaepernick became the team's starting quarterback, Crabtree became a favorite target. He had a career-high 1,105 yards receiving. He also had a great postseason and helped his team come within three points of a Super Bowl victory. In 2013 Crabtree had surgery for an ankle injury but still managed a career-high 14.9 yards per catch in the five games he played.

Year	Team	Games	Yards	Yds/Game	Yds/Catch	Receiving TDs
2009	SF	11	625	56.8	13.0	2
2010	SF	16	741	46.3	13.5	6
2011	SF	15	874	58.3	12.1	4
2012	SF	16	1,105	69.1	13.0	9
2013	SF	5	284	56.8	14.9	1

VICTOR CRUZ

The New York Giants had the ball on their own 1-yard line. The New York Jets had the lead in the December 2011 game and were looking to build on it. Giants quarterback Eli Manning dropped back deep into his own end zone and found wide receiver Victor Cruz running across the middle. Manning threw a hard pass. Cruz grabbed it. A defender stood ready to knock him down, but Cruz stopped, stepped backward, and let the tackler dive past him. Cruz ran up the sideline. He jumped over another defender and ran for the end zone. It was a 99-yard touchdown—the longest touchdown catch in Giants history. The amazing play gave the Giants a lead they would never give back.

Year	Team	Games	Yards	Yds/Game	Yds/Catch	Receiving TDs
2011	NYG	16	1,536	96.0	18.7	9
2012	NYG	16	1,092	68.3	12.7	10
2013	NYG	14	998	71.3	13.7	4

Cruz wasn't considered a big prospect coming out of the University of Massachusetts. He went undrafted in 2010 and signed with the New York Giants as a **free agent**. He barely made the team and didn't make a catch that year. In 2011 injuries forced the Giants to feature Cruz more. He didn't let his chance slip by. He had 82 receptions, piled up more than 1,500 yards receiving, and scored nine touchdowns. The following year, he scored 10 touchdowns and earned his first **Pro Bowl** appearance. Despite injuries that shortened his 2013 season, Cruz just missed the 1,000-yard mark in receiving for the third straight year.

free agent—a player who is free to sign with any team
Pro Bowl—the NFL's All-Star Game

The Denver Broncos were trailing the Kansas City Chiefs 7-0 going into the second quarter of a hard-fought 2013 game. Then Denver quarterback Peyton Manning and wide receiver Eric Decker found their groove. On first and 10 at the Chiefs' 41-yard line, Manning fired a perfect pass deep up the middle. Decker beat his defender and caught the pass for a touchdown. It was just the first of a career-high four-touchdown day for Decker and a 35-28 win for the Broncos. He finished the day with eight catches and 174 receiving yards.

Year	Team	Games	Yards	Yds/Game	Yds/Catch	Receiving TDs
2010	DEN	14	106	7.6	17.7	1
2011	DEN	16	612	38.3	13.9	8
2012	DEN	16	1,064	66.5	12.5	13
2013	DEN	16	1,288	80.5	14.8	11

Decker played football at the University of Minnesota, where he was also a baseball standout. He was drafted by the Denver Broncos in the third round of the 2010 draft, but he didn't play much on a team stacked with veteran wide receivers. Decker's role expanded in 2011, but he really exploded in 2012.

He caught 85 passes, scored 13 touchdowns, and established a strong bond with Denver's new quarterback, Peyton Manning. In 2013 Decker had a career-high 1,288 yards receiving and scored 11 touchdowns on the way to helping the Broncos to the Super Bowl.

JIMMY GRAHAM

The New Orleans Saints were trailing the Atlanta Falcons 17-13 in the opening game of the 2013 season. In the third quarter, the Saints started a drive on their own 20-yard line. As they moved up the field and got closer to a score, quarterback Drew Brees looked to tight end Jimmy Graham. On the Falcons' 14-yard line, Brees made a short pass to Graham, who gained seven yards and a first down.

It worked well the first time, so Brees and Graham tried it again. This time the duo combined for a touchdown. The Saints took the lead and ended up winning the game 23-17.

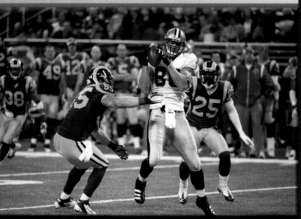

Graham was chosen by the Saints in the third round of the 2010 draft. Since then he has proven to be the best tight end in the NFL, posting numbers better than most wide receivers. Tight ends are often used as blockers, but Graham is a pass-catching machine. He had a monster year in 2011, racking up 1,310 receiving yards and 11 touchdowns. His 99 catches earned him the **franchise** record for receptions in a season. In 2013 he had a career-high 16 touchdowns, a total that set another franchise record and led the NFL among all receivers. The amazing season netted Graham All-Pro honors and his second Pro Bowl appearance.

Year	Team	Games	Yards	Yds/Game	Yds/Catch	Receiving TDs
2010	NO	15	356	23.7	11.5	5
2011	NO	16	1,310	81.9	13.2	11
2012	NO	15	982	65.5	11.6	9
2013	NO	16	1,215	75.9	14.1	16

franchise—team

GREEN

A.J. Green spent most of his 2011 NFL **debut** being shut down by the Cleveland Browns defense. When quarterback Andy Dalton left the game with an injury, it didn't seem like Green's fortunes would improve. Then, late in the fourth quarter, backup quarterback Bruce Gradkowski dropped back after a quick snap. Green streaked down the sideline and found himself wide open. Gradkowski fired a deep pass to Green for a 41-yard touchdown. Green's first NFL catch not only netted his team six points and the lead, but it came against his team's in-state rival. The Bengals ended up stunning the Browns 27-17.

With a reputation for big plays at the University of Georgia, wide receiver A.J. Green was drafted fourth overall by the Cincinnati Bengals in 2011. Green had a great **rookie** season, but he emerged as a true star in 2012. He and quarterback Andy Dalton teamed up for 97 catches that year. Green not only pulled in 11 touchdowns, he exploded for 12 plays of 25 yards or more. Green's numbers improved again in 2013 with 98 catches for 1,426 yards and 11 touchdowns. His stellar play helped the Bengals to the playoffs and sent him to his third Pro Bowl in as many years. Though he's a big man, Green has sneaky speed and the ability to out leap just about anyone.

Year	Team	Games	Yards	Yds/Game	Yds/Catch	Receiving TDs
2011	CIN	15	1,057	70.5	16.3	7
2012	CIN	16	1,350	84.4	13.9	11
2013	CIN	16	1,426	89.9	14.6	11

debut—a player's first appearance at a particular level
rookie—a first-year player

PERCY HARVIN

The Minnesota Vikings were facing their bitter rivals, the Green Bay Packers, for the second time in 2009. Minnesota quarterback Brett Favre dropped back in the third quarter and found wide receiver Percy Harvin in the middle of the field. One defender was trailing him, and two others were coming toward him, but Favre gunned the ball into the crowd. Harvin juked back, leaped up, and grabbed the ball while all three defenders collided and fell to the turf. After that it was an easy run to the end zone for a 51-yard touchdown.

Year	Team	Games	Yards	Yds/Game	Yds/Catch	Receiving TDs
2009	MIN	15	790	52.7	13.2	6
2010	MIN	14	868	62.0	12.2	5
2011	MIN	16	967	60.4	11.1	6
2012	MIN	9	677	75.2	10.9	3
2013	SEA	1	17	17.0	17.0	0

Harvin is explosive, powerful, and one of the hardest receivers to bring down. Mostly working out of the slot, he routinely turns short passes into big gains. In college he led the Florida Gators to two national titles. In 2009, his first year in the pros, he and the Vikings were just one game away from the Super Bowl.

Harvin was traded to the Seattle Seahawks after the 2012 season. He underwent hip surgery and was out for most of the 2013 season. Harvin came back to help the Seahawks to their first Super Bowl victory by returning a kickoff 87 yards for a touchdown and adding 45 receiving yards.

ANDRE JOHNSON

The Houston Texans made the postseason for the first time in franchise history in January 2012. Due to injuries, they started third-string quarterback T.J. Yates against the Cincinnati Bengals. But with seasoned pros such as wide receiver Andre Johnson as targets, the Texans knew they had a chance. With his team up by a touchdown in the third quarter, Johnson lined up wide left. Yates dropped back and threw a **bomb** down the left sideline. A wide-open Johnson moved easily under the ball for the catch and ran into the end zone. After nine years without tasting the playoffs, Johnson celebrated his first career postseason touchdown by leaping into the stands.

Year	Team	Games	Yards	Yds/Game	Yds/Catch	Receiving TDs
2003	HOU	16	976	61.0	14.8	4
2004	HOU	16	1,142	71.4	14.5	6
2005	HOU	13	688	52.9	10.9	2
2006	HOU	16	1,147	71.7	11.1	5
2007	HOU	9	851	94.6	14.2	8
2008	HOU	16	1,575	98.4	13.7	8
2009	HOU	16	1,569	98.1	15.5	9
2010	HOU	13	1,216	93.5	14.1	8
2011	HOU	7	492	70.3	14.9	2
2012	HOU	16	1,598	99.9	14.3	4
2013	HOU	16	1,407	87.9	12.9	5

A big man with speed to spare, Johnson has explosive skills to go with veteran smarts. As a star wide receiver at the University of Miami, he led the Hurricanes to an undefeated season and a national championship. Drafted third overall by the Texans in 2003, Johnson went to his first of seven Pro Bowls in 2004. He was named an All-Pro in 2008 and 2009 and led the league in receiving yards both years. He finished second in the NFL in receiving yards in 2012. He tallied more than 1,400 yards receiving the following year and caught five touchdowns.

bomb—a very long pass

CALVIN JOHNSON

In the fourth quarter of a 2012 game against the Atlanta Falcons, Detroit Lions quarterback Matthew Stafford took the shotgun snap and stepped back. Receiver Calvin Johnson ran a shallow crossing **route** into the middle of the field. When he looked in, Stafford's throw was on its way. Johnson caught it in the cradle of his right elbow and continued crossing the field, angling for more yardage. When he ran out of bounds after a 26-yard gain, Johnson owned the NFL single-season record for receiving yards. The crowd cheered wildly as Johnson ran to his coach for a hug and to have him hold on to the record-setting football.

Year	Team	Games	Yards	Yds/Game	Yds/Catch	Receiving TDs
2007	DET	15	756	50.4	15.8	4
2008	DET	16	1,331	83.2	17.1	12
2009	DET	14	984	70.3	14.7	5
2010	DET	15	1,120	74.7	14.5	12
2011	DET	16	1,681	105.1	17.5	16
2012	DET	16	1,964	122.8	16.1	5
2013	DET	14	1,492	106.6	17.8	12

Calvin Johnson has it all—size, strength, speed, great hands, and off-the-chart athleticism. Johnson was drafted second overall in 2007 by the Lions out of Georgia Tech. With four Pro Bowls and two receiving yard titles, it's clear that opposing defenses are having trouble stopping the man nicknamed Megatron. In 2012 Johnson caught 122 passes for 1,964 yards, breaking the single-season record previously held by the great Jerry Rice. The next season he averaged a career-high 17.8 yards per catch and posted more than 100 yards per game. When his impressive career is finally done, he just might challenge Jerry Rice as the best wide receiver to play the game.

route—the path a receiver runs after a play begins

JULIO
JONES

The Atlanta Falcons faced the San Francisco 49ers in the 2012 conference championship. In the first quarter alone, receiver Julio Jones racked up 100 yards and a touchdown. Atlanta had the ball on San Francisco's 20-yard line in the second quarter with Jones lined up wide to the left. Falcons quarterback Matt Ryan took the snap as Jones bolted down the left sideline. Ryan lofted a perfect pass into the back corner of the end zone. The defender was draped on Jones like a superhero's cape, but it didn't matter. Jones leaped, grabbed the ball, and came down with one foot in bounds. He dragged his other foot across the green turf as he fell forward for his second touchdown.

Jones is tall, strong, and a deep threat who gives defenses nightmares. As a sophomore at the University of Alabama, he helped his team win a BCS National Championship. After his junior year, Jones entered the 2011 NFL draft and was chosen with the sixth overall pick by the Falcons.

In Jones' first two seasons, he had a total of 18 receiving touchdowns, helping the Falcons to the playoffs both years. A foot injury ended Jones' 2013 season early, though it looked as if he was going to have a monster year. In just five games, he averaged a career-high 116 yards per game.

Year	Team	Games	Yards	Yds/Game	Yds/Catch	Receiving TDs
2011	ATL	13	959	73.8	17.8	8
2012	ATL	16	1,198	74.9	15.2	10
2013	ATL	5	580	116	14.1	2

DEMARYIUS THOMAS

The Denver Broncos' 2012 playoff game against the Pittsburgh Steelers was tied at 23. Broncos receiver Demaryius Thomas already had 124 receiving yards in the game, including catches for 58 and 51 yards. On the first play from **scrimmage** in overtime, the Steelers' defense lined up tight to defend against the run. Quarterback Tim Tebow faked a handoff, then threw a quick pass to Thomas who was slanting across the middle. Thomas caught it in stride and kept running. A defender closed in, but Thomas knocked him away with a stiff arm. Boom! Thomas turned on the jets and ran 80 yards for his first postseason touchdown and a big win for the Broncos.

scrimmage—an imaginary line where play begins

Year	Team	Games	Yards	Yds/Game	Yds/Catch	Receiving TDs
2010	DEN	10	283	28.3	12.9	2
2011	DEN	11	551	50.1	17.2	4
2012	DEN	16	1,434	89.6	15.3	10
2013	DEN	16	1,430	89.4	15.5	14

Fast and physical, Thomas is a powerhouse receiver who is not afraid to fight defensive backs for the ball or for extra yards after the catch. That bruising style helps him break big plays, even when it looks like he has nowhere to go. When superstar quarterback Peyton Manning came to Denver in 2012, Thomas' stats skyrocketed. He had a career-high 94 catches, 18 of which went for at least 25 yards. With equally impressive numbers and a career-high 14 touchdowns in 2013, Thomas helped his team reach the Super Bowl.

When the Indianapolis Colts faced the New England Patriots in 2009, fans knew it would be a high-scoring game. The Patriots had a 17-point lead early in the fourth quarter, but the Colts battled back. With 20 seconds left in the game and New England leading 34-28, the Colts lined up just one yard from the Patriots' end zone. Quarterback Peyton Manning took the snap as receiver Reggie Wayne got off the line and ran for the middle of the end zone. Manning hit him with a laser throw, and Wayne hauled it in. Touchdown, Colts! Wayne's second touchdown catch of the game had sealed the victory. The game has been called one of the best regular-season games of all time.

Year	Team	Games	Yards	Yds/Game	Yds/Catch	Receiving TDs
2001	IND	13	345	26.5	12.8	0
2002	IND	16	716	44.8	14.6	4
2003	IND	16	838	52.4	12.3	7
2004	IND	16	1,210	75.6	15.7	12
2005	IND	16	1,055	65.9	12.7	5
2006	IND	16	1,310	81.9	15.2	9
2007	IND	16	1,510	94.4	14.5	10
2008	IND	16	1,145	71.6	14.0	6
2009	IND	16	1,264	79.0	12.6	10
2010	IND	16	1,355	84.7	12.2	6
2011	IND	16	960	60.0	12.8	4
2012	IND	16	1,355	84.7	12.8	5
2013	IND	7	503	71.9	13.2	2

Known for his steady hands and precise route-running, Reggie Wayne is a veteran who never seems to grow old. After playing four years at the University of Miami, Wayne was drafted in 2001 by the Colts. He got to play with stars such as quarterback Peyton Manning and fellow wide receiver Marvin Harrison. Wayne had 27 catches as a rookie and nearly doubled that total his next year. He quickly became one of Manning's favorite targets. From 2004 to 2012, he had more than 1,000 yards receiving each season except one. In the 13 years he has been on the team, the Colts have missed the playoffs only twice. They've been to the Super Bowl twice and won it once.

WES WELKER

The New England Patriots led the Miami Dolphins 31-17 on opening day 2011. But the Dolphins made a defensive stand in the fourth quarter, pinning the Patriots deep in their own territory. As quarterback Tom Brady took the snap from the 1-yard line, the Dolphins came at him with a **blitz**. Brady quickly lofted a pass over the shoulder of a streaking Wes Welker. The sure-handed wide receiver caught the ball in stride, shook off the cornerback, and cruised 99 yards for the touchdown. The amazing play tied the record for the longest touchdown reception in NFL history.

Year	Team	Games	Yards	Yds/Game	Yds/Catch	Receiving TDs
2005	MIA	16	434	27.1	15.0	0
2006	MIA	16	687	42.9	10.3	1
2007	NE	16	1,175	73.4	10.5	8
2008	NE	16	1,165	72.8	10.5	3
2009	NE	14	1,348	96.3	11.0	4
2010	NE	15	848	56.5	9.9	7
2011	NE	16	1,569	98.1	12.9	9
2012	NE	16	1,354	84.6	11.5	6
2013	DEN	13	778	59.8	10.7	10

Welker is a reliable offensive force known for catching passes—lots of passes. Welker joined the Miami Dolphins in 2005. He returned kickoffs, returned punts, caught passes, and even kicked a field goal! But he really became a star when he was traded to the New England Patriots in 2007. His receptions spiked to 112 that year, and he had more than 1,100 yards receiving. He had a career-high 1,569 receiving yards and nine touchdowns in 2011. The five-time Pro Bowler and two-time All Pro joined the Denver Broncos in 2013. Welker's career-high 10 touchdowns helped Denver reach the Super Bowl.

blitz—a play in which a defender who does not normally rush the quarterback does so

Glossary

blitz—a play in which a defender who does not normally rush the quarterback does so

bomb—a very long pass

debut—a player's first appearance at a particular level

draft—the system by which NFL teams select new players

franchise—team

free agent—a player who is free to sign with any team

Pro Bowl—the NFL's All-Star Game

rookie—a first-year player

route—the path a receiver runs after a play begins

scrimmage—an imaginary line where a play begins

shotgun—the position from which the quarterback receives the ball a few feet behind the line of scrimmage instead of taking it directly from the center's hands

snap—the act of the center putting the football in play from the line of scrimmage

Der, Bob, ed. *Sports Illustrated Kids Big Book of Who Football.* New York: Time Home Entertainment Inc., 2013.

Frederick, Shane. *The Best of Everything Football Book.* All-Time Best of Sports. Mankato, Minn.: Capstone Press, 2011.

Wilner, Barry. *The Best NFL Receivers of All Time.* NFL's Best Ever. Minneapolis: ABDO Pub. Co., 2013.

Internet Sites

FactHound offers a safe, fun way to find Internet sites related to this book. All of the sites on FactHound have been researched by our staff.

Here's all you do:

Visit *www.facthound.com*

Type in this code: 9781491407608

Super-cool stuff!

Check out projects, games and lots more at
www.capstonekids.com